HAPPY HUBBY'S GUIDE TO MAKING YOUR WOMAN HAPPY TOO

SIX STEPS TO A BETTER RELATIONSHIP

Harvey Caras

Bloomington, IN   Milton Keynes, UK

authorHOUSE®

AuthorHouse™
1663 Liberty Drive, Suite 200
Bloomington, IN 47403
www.authorhouse.com
Phone: 1-800-839-8640

AuthorHouse™ UK Ltd.
500 Avebury Boulevard
Central Milton Keynes, MK9 2BE
www.authorhouse.co.uk
Phone: 08001974150

First published by AuthorHouse   12/13/2006

ISBN: 978-1-4259-6770-3 (sc)

Printed in the United States of America
Bloomington, Indiana

This book is printed on acid-free paper.

For Joanne

I hit life's lottery and you were the winning ticket

For
Jonathan, Rachel, Mickey, Sarah, and Dan

May you all enjoy a loving relationship
like Mom and I have

In Loving Memory

Vivian and Ernie Caras
Happy Together Again

TABLE OF CONTENTS

FOREWORD

A few years ago I got a call from Roger, an old friend who asked me to join him for dinner. Since guys don't call guys just to invite them to dinner, my first inclination was that Roger wanted to sell me something. So I showed up for the dinner prepared with all of the excuses I thought I would need to avoid buying whatever it was he was selling.

We ordered drinks and, much to my surprise, Roger began the conversation like this:

"Next month is my 25ᵗʰ wedding anniversary. I know I could just go out and buy my wife more jewelry, but this year I want to give her something even better. I want to become a better husband. I want to make my wife happier than she has ever been. And that is why I am talking to you!"

"Of all the husbands I know, you seem to be the one who knows the most about making your wife happy. So I would like to learn your secrets."

Needless to say I was flattered by Roger's request.

Joanne and I have been together for over 25 years, and she certainly is the happiest person I know. But I had never talked to anyone about how the things I did contributed to her happiness.

For three hours my friend and I sat as he listened to me talk about my philosophies on making a woman happy. He thanked me profusely and pledged to implement many of my suggestions.

About six months later I ran into Roger's wife Susan at a dinner party. She quickly pulled me aside and hugged me.

"Thank you for all the things that you taught my husband," she said. "I have never been happier in my life. Our marriage is stronger than it has ever been, and my husband is a lot happier too!"

And then Susan hit me with a suggestion that I had never considered.

"You know, you really ought to write a book!"

So here it is.

INTRODUCTION

Chances are that you either bought this book for yourself or it was given to you by the woman in your life. Okay, maybe your kids gave it to you but if they did it was probably because of a "strong suggestion" by their mother!

If you bought the book for yourself then I do not need to convince you to keep reading. If, however the book was handed to you by someone you love then you may be asking the following two questions:

"Who is this guy and why should I pay attention to what he has to say?"

These are both very legitimate questions.

Let me start with what I am NOT.

I am not Dr. Phil.

I am not a psychologist, psychiatrist, or anything else with "psych" attached to it.

In my professional career I teach people how to get along better and resolve disputes in the workplace.

My clients include Armstrong, Alcoa, BASF, Dana, Dupont, Ford, Kodak, Marriott, Mattel, International Paper, GE, Toyota, Universal Studios, and hundreds of other companies.

Along the way I have learned a lot about people and relationships.

And I have also learned a lot about how to make a woman happy!

Where did I learn this?

I grew up in a house where my father adored my mother and she was the happiest woman I knew.

Were we rich? Not even close. My dad had a little corner variety store that went "belly-up" when he was 48. By my calculations he never earned more than $20,000 in any one year of his life.

Did we have a lot of material possessions? No, just the basics, a house, car, food and clothes

Did we travel a lot? Not unless you count our five mile trips to the beach on summer Sundays.

So then why was my mother so happy?

My mother was happy because my father made her happiness his most important job.

And he was really good at it.

It was that simple.

People used to say that, for Ernie Caras, the heavens opened up one day and sent him his angel named Vivian.

And that is how he treated her every single day.

I remember my dad telling me once, *"The greatest gift a man can give to his children is to love their mother and make her happy."*

I have been married to Joanne for well over twenty years, and we are happier today than we were on our honeymoon. We have had three kids together, suffered illnesses together, buried three of our parents together, watched our house burn down and destroy everything we owned together. We have laughed together and cried together. But most of all we have stayed together. And every day I thank the lord that I have been so lucky in life.

Now it is time for some truth in advertising.

Joanne is my second wife.

My first wife and I divorced after ten years of marriage. She is a great lady who deserved a better husband than I was to her.

You see, in my first marriage I did whatever I thought would make me happy, not my wife.

I did not follow my father's methods in my first marriage because I thought that my dad was a wimp who sacrificed his own life just to please my mother.

I looked at the things he did and they did not fit the image I had of "real men" from movies and TV.

John Wayne would never do that stuff.

Clint Eastwood would never say those things.

There was no way I was going to do that stuff or say those things either!

What a fool I was.

It wasn't until my first marriage ended that I began to take a second look at my dad.

It was pretty easy to see that he was a lot happier than I was!

It was then that I realized that the best way for any man to be happy himself is to live with a happy woman. And conversely the fastest route to personal misery is to live with an unhappy woman!

So when my dad said that making my mom happy was his most important job, I finally understood why!

I was determined that my second marriage would be better than my first. So I asked my dad to spell out his philosophy and ideas to me.

And that is how I learned most of the tips I am going to give you in this book.

Does all of this qualify me to write a book? You will judge that for yourself, but hopefully not until after you have read what I have to say.

This book is based on a very simple philosophy:

If you make your woman happy then your life will be happy.

Make her happiness your number one goal and you will be even happier.

What goes around comes around!

So in reality it is a very self serving thing you do when you make your woman happy.

I learned most of what is in this book from my dad, but I realized that he was not the only man in the world who knew how to make his woman happy. So I have spent the past year talking to men and women from all walks of life, studying the things that men did to make women happy.

I have put my suggestions in to a series of steps that you can follow to make life happier for your lady and for yourself too.

They will help you build a better relationship.

Nobody will do everything suggested in this book, not even me!

In my professional career I teach a leadership course to managers and supervisors of major corporations. Before the class begins I tell them that, while we will be together for eight hours, I hope that each of them will get their "ten minutes worth" from my workshop. By that I mean that I want each of them to take a few things from the workshop that they will put to use in their daily life.

I feel the same way about this book, and I suggest that you will find your "ten minutes worth" in the following pages.

My genuine hope is that you will try a few of these ideas. If they work for you I hope that you will pass them on to your sons.

STEP ONE

Tell Her Again and
Again and Again

*"Tell her you love her each day,
you'll make her happy that way.
A simple "I love you" means more than money,
and with a kiss or two her life is sunny."*

Frank Sinatra

Do you remember the movie "Ghost" with Demi Moore and Patrick Swayzie? A famous running line throughout the move was that every time Demi would say "I love you" to Patrick his response was always "Ditto".

For some reason, old Patrick just couldn't bring himself to say the words "I love you." And Demi was so in love with him that she was perfectly fine with that.

I find that hard to believe.

But then again, that movie also asked us to believe that Patrick died and came back to Demi as a ghost who could only talk to his wife through the body of Whoopie Goldberg.

So I had to suspend disbelief, which left me free to accept the whole *"I love you"* debacle as well.

I believe that every woman wants to be told that she is loved, as often as possible.

If your woman says that it doesn't matter that much to her she is probably just protecting herself against the disappointment of not hearing it enough.

The words *"I love you"* are an expression of feelings. Conventional wisdom tells us that many men have a difficult time expressing their feelings. I believe that is nonsense!

Let me give you some expressions of feelings that men are perfectly willing to share:

    "I'm exhausted!"
    "I'm hungry"
    "I'm horny"

"She's hot!"
"Damn that p***es me off!"
"Great shot!"
"Those (fill in the team) broke my heart again!"

All of these expressions seem to flow easily from the lips of men, but for some men the words "I love you" are as difficult as a colonoscopy.

I remember the story of my old friend Tony who once told me that he had one major regret in his life. Several years ago he and his wife had a little spat and she left the house in a huff. An hour later he got a call from the police telling him that she had been killed in a car accident.

For the rest of his life Tony regretted that he had no chance to tell his wife that he loved her before she died.

So from that day forward Tony made a point to tell everyone who was special to him, including of course his new wife Judy, whom he married several years later, that he loved them. Tony ended every conversation, whether it was on the phone or in person, with the words "I love you."

Last year Tony died suddenly of a heart attack.

At his funeral Judy spoke eloquently about the loving man that Tony was. She told us how he always said

"I love you" to her. And those were the last words she ever heard from him, words that will stay with her forever.

So here is advice number one from Happy Hubby. Say "I love you" to your woman all the time!

Say it when you wake up in the morning.

Say it when you leave for work.

Say it at the end of every phone call.

Say it before you fall asleep.

Say it on her birthday.

Say it on your anniversary.

Say it when it is not her birthday or your anniversary.

She may be surprised to hear it so often at first, especially if you have not said it too much in the past. But I promise you that she will get used to it. And she will love it!

The only way to get more comfortable with the expression of love is to use it a lot. After all, if a golfer has difficulty with sand traps, the best way to get better is to practice.

And while you are doing that you can also practice on your kids, your parents, and even your siblings. You will be amazed at the response you get. My guess is that eventually these people will say "I love you too."

If they say *"ditto"* you can bet they have the seen the movie "Ghost".

Once you have become comfortable with the words "I love you" you can begin to add the word "because".

The movie "When Harry met Sally" had a famous line where Billy Crystal (Harry) tells Meg Ryan (Sally) for the first time that he loves her. I may not have the exact words here but it went something like this:

"I know I love you because you are the last person I want to talk to before I go to bed at night and you are the first person I want to see when I wake up in the morning".

That is one of the best lines ever used in a movie to express love. Unfortunately the line was overshadowed in the movie by the scene in the restaurant when Sally shows Harry how easy it is for a woman to fake an orgasm. Right after this amazingly sexy display a woman at a nearby table tells her waitress "I'll have what she's having!"

Women not only want to be loved but they also want to hear why they are loved.

*"I love you **because** you are my best friend in the whole world"*

*"I love you **because** you always make me feel special."*

*"I love you **because** you are such a wonderful mother to our children."*

*"I love you **because** you make me a better person."*

*"I love you **because** you are as beautiful on the inside as you are on the outside."*

*"I love you **because** you have a heart as big as the whole outdoors."*

*"I love you **because** you have taught me how to love."*

Feel free to use any of the above expressions, but I bet that if you put your mind to it you can come up with your own ideas. After all, the more genuine and personal they are the more meaning they will have to the woman in your life.

Once you get really good at this you can begin to quantify your love.

Remember the famous line from "Romeo and Juliet"?

"How do I love thee? Let me count the ways."

Here is an updated version:

"Honey, do you know how much I love you? I love you so much that if you took all the grains of sand at the beach and all of the drops of water in the ocean and added them all up it still wouldn't equal the size of my love for you."

Sounds corny? Maybe so.

But ask yourself a question. Is it true? Do I love this woman that much?

If the answer is "yes" then why not tell her?

She will love it!

Here are a few other examples of love quantified:

*"**I love you** more than words can possibly describe."*

*"**I love you** with every ounce of strength that I have in my body."*

*"**I love you** more than I ever thought it was possible to love."*

"I love you more today than yesterday…but not as much as tomorrow!"

"Thank you for loving me!"

Recently my daughter Rachel and her boyfriend Dan were reading Cosmopolitan Magazine together. The article mentioned that the average man falls in love at least seven times over the course of his lifetime. Since Rachel and Dan were High School sweethearts this fact deeply concerned my daughter.

"I am worried about this" Rachel said sadly to Dan.

Dan's reply was as swift as it was perfect:

"Rachel, I fall in love with you every single day!"

Somebody taught that young man well.

So this chapter can be summarized in one simple sentence.

Step one to making your woman happy is to tell her that you love her, why you love her, and how much you love her as often as possible.

STEP TWO

Rekindle the Romantic Flame

Buy me a rose, call me from work
Open a door for me, what would it hurt
Show me you love me by the look in your eyes
These are the little things I need the most in my life

Luther Vandross

Think back to when you first started dating the lady in your life.

Can you recall the feeling you had when you thought about this fantastic person you had recently met?

Remember how your heart raced before you picked up the phone to call her?

Relive the feelings that you had the first time you kissed her.

Now think about all of the sweet little things you did to let her know how much she meant to you.

When was the last time you did those little things?

My advice is that you start the dating process all over again. Imagine yourself in the early romantic stages of your relationship with her and begin doing the kinds of things you did back then.

Hold doors open for her.

Drop her off at the door and then go park the car.

Hold the umbrella over her when it rains.

Call her on the phone just to say *"hi"*.

Grasp her hand when you walk together.

Hug her as often as possible.

Remember those days and you will remember how happy you were.

Here are a few sure fire romantic things that you can do to rekindle the romance in your relationship:

Go Out On "Dates"

My friends Howard and Lori have been married for well over 30 years, and for the past several years they have had a "date" every Thursday afternoon.

Their dates usually consist of a movie, an art gallery, or a museum, followed by a quiet dinner in a nice restaurant.

So when anyone asks Howard how long they have been married he says "We've been married for thirty years, and we've been dating for ten!"

These "dates" can be especially romantic if they are planned in advance. Just as a newly dating couple takes the time to look for something special that will interest both of them, so too can a long term couple, married or not.

Give Her a "No Occasion" Card

Every man on the planet knows enough to give his woman a sweet card for her birthday, Valentine's Day, your anniversary, Christmas, and possibly Mother's Day. Some may even consider those an obligation. So what about the other 360 days of the year? Are there any other days that are worthy of a card? I suggest that you pick a random day and buy your lady a card that says how much she means to you.

Give it to her when she wakes up in the morning. I guarantee you that it will have more impact on her than every other card you have ever bought.

The idea that you took the time to pick out a card with a special saying when you didn't have to do it will mean more to her than the card itself. Try it guys. This one is a guaranteed winner!

Bring Home Flowers

Flowers are nature's way of making the world a beautiful place. We all give them on special occasions. But why not stop on the side of the road one day and pick up a dozen roses for that special woman in your life? Hand them to her when you walk through the door.

I bet she will say *"What are these for?"*

With a smile your answer will be *"These are for the most wonderful girl in the world."*

Can't afford a dozen? One will mean just as much.

Draw Her Bath

Very few things make a woman feel better than a warm soothing bath. And the best baths of all are those drawn for them by the man in their life.

So try this one day. When your woman comes home from work have a warm bath waiting for her. Fill the tub with water and aromatic crystals. A copy of her favorite Woman's magazine waiting by the tub will make things even better. Have her favorite fuzzy slippers, negligee, and robe waiting for her. Order dinner over the phone and have it delivered.

Is this a request for sex? It doesn't have to be, because she will be as close to a "sure thing" as you can possibly want!

Pay Her a Compliment

Every time you open your mouth you have a choice to say something that makes people feel good or bad.

You can be positive or negative, complimentary or critical, supportive or deflating.

If the woman you love is the most important person in your life then it makes sense to always choose to be positive, complimentary, and supportive.

Every woman I know has at least one quality that they are proud of, some have many. If you know what your lady is most proud of then you need to let her know that you are proud of her too.

What does your lady feel most proud of? Is it something about her body? Her legs, her eyes, her hair?

Is it the way she devotes herself to your children?

Is it her success at work or in athletics?

How about the relationships she has with her family or friends?

If you are with a woman who takes no special pride in any aspect of her life then you need to let her know what makes her special to you.

If you tell her over and over again with sincerity what is special about her then eventually she will begin to feel the same way about herself.

Here are a few examples:

"Sweetheart, you have the most beautiful eyes I have ever seen. I fell in love with your eyes ten years ago and they still make me melt every time you walk into a room."

"Honey, there is nobody else on this planet that I would choose to be the mother of my children. All of us are so lucky to have you."

"It always amazes me how you are able to balance your career and your family. I know how tough it is for you

and I want you to know how much I appreciate all that you do."

"You have the ability to make people feel better about themselves whenever you speak. I truly admire that gift."

My friend Terese told me how her husband Roy gave her a compliment that made her feel good.

"Last night Roy said 'Honey, you look exactly the same as you did the day I met you!'

"I knew it was B.S. but I love him for saying it anyway!"

Tell Others How Great She Is

Letting your woman know how special she is to you is very important. But equally important is that you let other people know the same thing. Tell her friends, your friends, relatives, anybody who will listen, just how terrific the lady in your life is.

Tell them the story of how you first met and how your friendship blossomed into romance.

Trust me. It will get back to her. And the fact that you told others will be as important to her as the fact that you told her, maybe even more important.

Not only will her friends tell her how special she is to you, but they will also tell her what a great guy she is with!

What goes around comes around!

Display Your Affection in Public

The more you show the world know how much you love your lady the more loved she will feel.

Look for opportunities to show affection in front of others, such as:

- She is walking off the tennis courts with her friends. You are there waiting for her with a single red rose, a big hug, and a kiss.

- You are walking with your wife and children when all of sudden you stop and kiss your wife. *"Get a room you two!"* the kids will say. But they will always remember how much their dad loved their mom.

- You are out to dinner with several couples. As your lady is about to sit you move the chair for her, allow her to sit, then plant a gentle kiss on her forehead.

- You are dancing at a wedding when all of sudden you "dip" your lady and kiss her on the dance floor.

- You surprise her at work one day with a dozen roses.

Play Your Song

Do you have a favorite song that you share? The one that played on the radio the night you met or the song they played at your wedding?

Ours is called "One in A Million", by Larry Graham (a classic "one hit wonder").

Your song, whatever it may be, will always bring back memories to her of the most special day in her life.

So use the song to make her happy.

Here are a few ways to do that:

Buy the CD and secretly sneak it into her car. Add a little note on the steering wheel directing her to the CD and she will smile all the way to wherever she is driving.

Call her favorite radio station and dedicate the song to her. When they ask what the special occasion is tell them:

"Every day is special with her!"

Dolores and Larry have been married for eighteen years.

"One night Larry and I were driving home from dinner and our song came on the radio. It was dark and it was late but that didn't stop Larry."

'He turned up the volume on the radio. Then he pulled the car to the side of the road, opened the door for me and took me by the hand.

"We danced on the grass to our song while cars drove by honking at us. I have never felt more in love with this man than I did that night."

Make Her Breakfast in Bed

This one is so old that it has become a cliché. But breakfast in bed is still a sure fire winner in my book.

The key here is not to wait for a special occasion. Do it one morning after your lady has worked especially hard, or has completed an important task. Leave the breakfast by the bed with a personal note telling her how proud you are of what she has done.

Cuddle

Yes women do like to cuddle more than men. But that just means that you have another opportunity to make her happy!

You can cuddle in bed, while you watch TV, at the movies, or even in the car while you are waiting for someone. Look for every opportunity to pull her near to you and hold her.

Gently stroke her hair and kiss the top of her head.

By doing this you are saying (without words) "I love being close to you."

Rub Her Feet

I'm not sure what it is that makes women like having their feet massaged so much. Most men I know cannot stand to have their feet touched, but women seem to love it.

So here is a suggestion. One night while you are home watching TV remove your woman's shoes.

Gently but firmly massage her feet, starting with the heel and gradually working your way up to her toes.

She will let you know what feels the best, so you can concentrate on that.

Nothing needs to be said. Your hands and fingers will speak volumes about your love for her.

Just "Hang Out"

Driving together in the car to do daily errands may seem like a very mundane way to spend time but in actuality it can be one of the most romantic things a couple can do together.

What makes this so great is that, all the while they are driving around from errand to errand the man and woman are together in the car, alone!

No kids, no jobs, just the two of them. If the cell phones and radios are turned off this can be a fantastic opportunity for uninterrupted communication.

Want to make it even better?

Try telling your lady the following:

"Honey I would rather be doing nothing with you than anything else with anyone else!"

Find That Special Thing You Always Do For Her

Look for a little gesture that you can make on a regular basis that constantly reminds her how important she is to you, how protective you are of her, and also how important you are to her.

Whenever my mom would walk up or down a flight of stairs my dad would walk two steps below her.

"If she falls," he would say, *"I want to be there to catch her."*

Mom never fell but Dad was always there for her.

Ironically just a few years after Dad died my mom was visiting my house when she did fall down the steps, breaking her hip.

"I needed my Ernie to catch me" she said softly with tears in her eyes.

Here are a few examples of things you can do for your woman:

- Bring her morning coffee every day from the local convenience store "just the way she likes it".

- Bring home one red rose every Friday.

- Call her at the same time every day just to see how her day is going.

- Give her a day off from the kids every other Saturday so she can devote the day to herself.

- Make her popcorn every Sunday evening before you watch "Desperate Housewives" together.

- Say the same sweet thing to her every morning when she wakes up, or every night just before she falls asleep.

Go For Walks

Walking is a great way to find the time to be alone together.

Find a special place that you make "your spot" to walk. The more beautiful and natural the setting the more romantic it will be…a lake, a nature trail.

Use the time you walk together to rekindle the romance in your relationship. Here are a few things you can do to help make that happen:

- Stop and pick a flower for her to put in her hair.

- Hold hands.

- Reminisce about the happiest times you have had together.

- Dream about the future.

- Tell her how much you love her.

Do Something Playful

Every once in a while it is fun to act like little kids!

Joanne and I have a boat that we call our "yacht". We keep it in the garage at our home at Sea Colony in Bethany Beach, Delaware. Last year someone asked me how big the "yacht" was and I replied:

"I'm not exactly sure. I'll have to blow it up to measure it!"

At least once or twice each week my lady and I jump in the "yacht" on the pond behind our house and off we go.

I use one oar to row us nowhere as I sing bad love songs while Joanne drinks iced tea and laughs.

The neighbors often line up to take pictures of the two of us making complete fools of ourselves. Our friends Roy and Terese even went so far as to have our photo blown up and framed. They added a caption to the photo with the words to the song I was singing that day.

The funniest thing about the photo is that the boat looks like it is about to sink beneath me while Joanne, who is half my weight, is way up in the air. We look like we are on a seesaw!

Joanne says that the photo proves I need to lose a few pounds (which I do). But I, of course, insist that the "yacht" is defective.

Every time I look at that photo I realize how much fun two people can have together.

So don't be afraid to do something silly and fun. These are the little things that create memories for a lifetime!

Make Her Laugh

Almost every woman I spoke with said that one of the qualities she finds most attractive about her man is his sense of humor.

"He makes me laugh" is the line used most often.

Does this mean that you have to be Robin Williams or Jerry Seinfeld to make a woman happy?

Absolutely not.

But you can add greatly to her enjoyment of life and your own by looking for opportunities to make her laugh.

Here are a few suggestions on how to do this:

- If you watch great comedians they are not simply telling jokes. The real humor is in the twist they put on day to day activities.

- If you are not a naturally witty guy I suggest that you pay attention to your friends that are.

Watch how they are able to see the humor in things and then ask them for tips on how to do it yourself.

- Groucho Marx was the fastest wit I have ever seen. An urban legend has it that once on his television show "You Bet Your Life" he was interviewing a man who had ten children.

  "How did you end up with so many kids?" Groucho asked incredulously,

  "I love my wife!" was the man's terse reply.

  Groucho's response came back like a shot from a   pistol.

  "I love my cigar too," he quipped, *"but I take it out of my mouth once in a while!"*

- Look for an opportunity to tell stories that have a humorous edge. And as my dad used to say *"Never let the truth get in the way of a good story."*

- When I hear a funny story or joke that I want to tell Joanne I write it down immediately because I know that I am terrible at remembering the joke. Before I started doing that I would come home and say *"I heard a great joke today!"*

  "Oh good what was it?" she would always ask.

"I forgot!" was my normal reply.

Now I write them down!

- The internet is an endless source for funny jokes and stories. Try saving the ones that strike you as funny. Then either forward them to her or print them out and give them to her.

- If you find a funny cartoon in a magazine or newspaper cut it out and paste it on the bathroom mirror for her to see.

- Learn what your lady finds funny, what tickles her.

- Also learn what she finds offensive. Stay away from vulgar or racist jokes. And stay away from jokes that make her the target.

- Practical jokes are usually a turn off for women, so please, no water balloons!

- Self depreciating humor is the best of all. If you want a lesson on that kind of humor I suggest that you watch a tape of the late Rodney Dangerfield. He was the master. One of Rodney's great lines was "I get no respect!"

"My wife cut me back to sex once a month", he said. *"But I'm lucky because three other guys she cut off completely!"*

STEP THREE

Take a Perpetual Honeymoon

I could stay awake just to hear you breathing
Watch you smile while you are sleeping
While you're far away dreaming
I could spend my life in this sweet surrender
I could stay lost in this moment forever
Every moment spent with you is a moment I treasure

Aerosmith

Many couples look back on their honeymoon as the best vacation they ever had. Exhausted from their wedding, they were free to just lay back and relax, usually in some warm and exotic place, while being waited on day and night.

If only we could make that last a lifetime.

I am going to show you that you certainly can!

The problem that most married couples have is that when they go on "vacation" this is what they do.

They pack up their three kids, dog, and cat, and move them from their nice three-bedroom, three-bath home into a two- bedroom, one-bath condo near the ocean.

In my book that is not a "vacation".

That is called a trip!

Remember Chevy Chase and the rest of the Griswold family?

With grandma strapped to the roof of their car? Hilarious.

Now don't get me wrong. I am not dead set against family trips. It is just that they do nothing to strengthen the relationship between Mom and Dad. As a matter of fact, Mom and Dad usually have no time alone together, and by the end of the trip they are exhausted and can't wait to get home.

There is a time and a place for these trips, but in order to make your woman (and yourself) happy, you have to plan some time away for just the two of you.

If your kids are young it may be impossible to leave them with grandma for more than a few days at a time, but that is okay.

As a matter of fact, short "getaways" are the best and most romantic vacations of all.

Here is how to do it right.

Start by finding a place that caters to couples, not kids. The last thing you want to do is leave your kids at home so that you can share your vacation with somebody else's kids!

I remember making that mistake a few years ago when Joanne and I traveled to Myrtle Beach with our friends Ron and Karen.

We arrived at a fabulous condo overlooking a golf course and immediately headed for the pool.

Just as we had covered ourselves with the obligatory glob of sun tan lotion the trouble began.

He looked like an ordinary kid, two arms and two legs. But within minutes we realized that "Buddy" was a poster child for Attention Deficit Disorder.

For the rest of the week every moment we spent by the pool was consumed with watching Buddy do cannonball leaps and belly flops into the pool, splashing the entire pool area. He loved to use his ear piercing scream to scare and torture his younger siblings.

All the while his mom sat patiently saying *"Buddy don't do that!"*

Not once did she move a muscle to stop Buddy or even slow him down.

Finally she came up with the perfect solution to change Buddy's focus.

"Why don't you kids play "Marco Polo?" she suggested.

Just shoot me!

So remember to pick a place that does not allow anyone under twenty one. (I would suggest that you find a place that bans anyone under 40 but I think you might have a hard time finding one).

Then pick a place that is close enough to home so that you can get there quickly but not so close that you can be called home easily.

Now look for a place that has activities that you both enjoy. If you are a golfer and your wife is not, save the golf resort for the time you go away with your golfing buddies. This time pick a place that offers things that she likes to do.

Make sure that you eat every meal at a restaurant.

Have room service deliver breakfast in bed.

Do not try to save a few dollars by asking your wife to "whip something up in the condo" one evening.

The idea is to take her away from the things she does every day, not simply move them.

Tell the resort ahead of time that it is a special occasion. (You have my permission to make one up).

Hopefully this "special occasion" will insure that you get a great room and a little extra V.I.P. treatment.

Now here is the most important part of the whole package. Plan a series of activities that will let her know how much she is loved. Spa treatments will pamper her body. Champagne with dinner and romantic music will relax her mind. Dancing to special songs will open her heart.

For a really romantic treat schedule "his and hers" massages.

Make this "honeymoon" the best few days of her life, and she will make them great for you too.

Honeymoon at home

Okay so maybe you can't afford the time or the money to take "getaway vacations".

Believe it or not there is good news for you too.

You can plan all of the same activities without ever leaving your home.

First you need to get the kids out of the house, for one night or as many as you can beg people to accommodate.

Once that is accomplished you need to plan a special "home getaway" just for the two of you.

Start by sending your lady an "invitation" to be your guest for the night. Give her a schedule of activities and a menu for dinner.

Here are a few suggestions to make this one of the best nights of her life (and yours)

Take a bath together

Did you ever watch animals groom each other? That seems to be a natural instinct for many animal species, so why not humans?

One of the most loving and tender things a couple can do is to take a hot bath together. Nothing beats a large heart shaped tub with mirrors on the ceiling, but since you probably don't have one of those in your house I would suggest you just use whatever you've got.

Fill the tub with hot water and be sure to shave before you get in.

Throw a few rose petals into the water, along with her favorite bath oil.

Lower the lights in the room, using candles to set the mood. Play romantic music (see below for suggestions). Then pour each of you a glass of champagne.

When you were eighteen you probably would have been groping the girl from the moment you got in the tub. And the whole "event" would most likely have been over in seconds.

But now you are a man in control of yourself, so take your time and savor every moment of the bath.

Wash her body from head to toe; stopping to pay extra attention to the places that feel the best.

And don't forget to wash her hair!

I doubt if I have to continue with advice from this point on, but just remember that your main goal is to be romantic and loving. Let the rest happen naturally.

Watch a Romantic Movie Together

There is no better way to have a romantic "in house honeymoon" than to put on your pajamas and cuddle up in front of the television set with a blanket and a great romantic movie.

Here are some of the best and most romantic movies you can rent and watch together.

And don't forget the popcorn!

Don Juan Demarco

Johnny Depp stars as a young man whom women find irresistible. (Perfect type casting according to Joanne). He teaches Marlon Brando and Faye Dunaway how to rekindle the romance in their marriage. The sex appeal in this movie is overwhelming for most women. This movie is as close to a "sure thing" as you can possibly get!

And the theme song of the movie, by Bryan Adams, has one of the most romantic lines in song history:

*"When you can see your unborn children in her eyes…
you know you really love a woman!"*

Romance rating: 5 hearts (out of 5)

When Harry Met Sally

Meg Ryan and Billy Crystal take the entire movie to
figure out that they can be best friends and lovers at
the same time. This movie is funny and touching and
offers some great insight into the relationship between
a man and a woman. Several times during the movie
random couples are featured on a sofa talking about
how they met and how much they love each other.

Romance rating: 4 hearts

Pretty Woman

Richard Gere hires Julia Roberts to be his "date" for
a week, and they end up falling in love. Once you
get past the thought of Richard Gere having to pay
for companionship and Julia Roberts as a hooker this
becomes a great movie.

Romance rating: 4 hearts

50 First dates

After an auto accident causes Drew Barrymore to lose
her memory every night Adam Sandler comes along

and falls in love with her. The problem is that he has to make her fall in love with him all over again every single day. How he does it makes for a delightful and romantic movie.

Romance Rating: 5 hearts

Sleepless in Seattle

Tom Hanks is a widower whose son writes a letter to a radio station. When hopeless romantic Meg Ryan hears the letter read over the airwaves she falls in love with Hanks. The ironic part of this movie is that the couple never meets each other until the very end!

Romance Rating: 4 hearts

An Affair to Remember

Cary Grant and Debra Kerr star in this classic movie about a couple who meet by chance and then agree to meet again six months later at the Empire State Building. Dire circumstances keep her from going but somehow they find a way back into each others arms.

This movie was remade with Warren Beatty and Annette Benning, but the original is still the best.

Romance rating: 5 hearts

The Notebook

James Garner stars as an elderly man who lives in a nursing home to be with the woman he loves, Gina Rowlands. Flashbacks of their life together are steamy and romantic. And the ending will knock your socks off (and probably the rest of your clothes too!)

Romance Rating: 5 hearts

While You Were Sleeping

Sandra Bullock is a subway token seller who falls for a man she sees every day but has never spoken with. Then after he is injured and unconscious she is mistaken for his fiancé.

Does she end up with the man of her dreams? Yes but it turns out to be the brother.

Romance rating: 4 hearts

Ghost

Patrick Swayzie stars as a man who dies and comes back to earth as a ghost. The touching and romantic scenes between Patrick and his wife, Demi Moore, are as wonderful after his death as they are before.

Romance rating: 4 hearts

Somewhere in Time

This was the best role ever for the late Christopher Reeve. He stars as a young playwright who meets an old woman in the theater one day.

"Come back to me!" she implores, and he is smitten.

Magically he is drawn to a beautiful old inn where he is transported back in time to meet Jane Seymour, the girl of his dreams.

This movie takes romance to its greatest level ever

Romance rating: 5 hearts plus!!

Movies NOT to see together

  The Godfather (parts 1, 2, or 3)

  Goodfellas

  Any boxing movie (except maybe Rocky I)

  Any Kung Fu movie

  Unfaithful

  Any movie starring Arnold Schwarzenegger

  (Except maybe True Lies with Jamie Lee Curtis)

  The Piano

Animal House

Any movie with Ben Stiller, Vin Diesel,
Carrot Top, or Pauly Shore

Romantic Music

Music is, of course, a matter of personal taste. Some like rock, some like rap, and others like country.

But certain songs transcend genre and tell timeless stories of romance and love.

They appeal to all ages, men and women of all backgrounds.

Here are a few CD's that should become part of your collection:

- Rod Stewart- It Had to Be You
- Rod Stewart- As Time Goes By
- Rod Stewart- Stardust
- Frank Sinatra- The Very Best Of
- Tony Bennett-All Time Greatest Hits
- Michael Buble- Michael Buble
- Harry Connick Jr.- We Are in Love
- Harry Connick Jr.- Only You
- Soundtrack- Sleepless in Seattle
- Soundtrack- When Harry Met Sally
- Luther Vandross- The Very Best Of Love
- Nat King Cole- Greatest Hits

- Celine Dion- Let's Talk About Love
- Anything from Kenny G
- Soundtrack-Somewhere In Time
- Bryan Adams- The Best Of Me
- Marvin Gaye- Greatest Hits

STEP FOUR

Shower Her with Gifts

I can only give you love that lasts forever
And a promise to be there each time you call
And the only heart I own
For you and you alone
That's all, that's all

Rod Stewart

If you have not read the forward to this book I would like you to read it now.

Go ahead I will wait for you to come back!

Remember what my friend Roger said about his wife?

"I know I could just go out and buy my wife more jewelry, but this year I want to give her something even better."

Remember how he asked for my advice on becoming a better husband? And how we talked for three hours as I shared my philosophy on how to make a woman happy?

Here is what is not in the foreword.

At the very end of the conversation Roger asked me if I had any other advice for him.

"Just one more thing," I said.

"Buy her the jewelry!"

We will discuss jewelry later in this chapter, but the important thing to keep in mind is that gifts come in all price ranges. You do not have to be wealthy to shower a woman with gifts. You simply need to know when, how, and what to give her.

Knowing what to buy and how much to spend is, in some ways, an art form.

Recently my friend Rob went into a gift shop and was looking around when an attractive young sales clerk asked if she could help him.

"I'm not sure what to buy." Rob offered.

"Well let's start with how much you want to spend, "the young lady replied.

Rob was quick to offer his thoughts on the subject. *"I want to spend as little as it takes to have sex tonight."*

After observing the stunned look on the sales clerk's face Rob quickly realized his faux pas.

"Not with you!" he shouted

Neither Rob nor his wife ever told me the end of the story, so I'm not sure if he bought the "right thing" or not, but I suspect that he did

So how does a man know what to buy his lady?

First let's start with the basics.

Almost every woman would be happy to receive any of the following from her man:

Jewelry

Perfume

Flowers

Lingerie

Jewelry

Did I say jewelry twice?

Yes I did, and that was not a typo!

What kind of jewelry is best for your lady? That's difficult to say, but easy to find out.

My advice is that you browse jewelry stores with her occasionally and see what things she likes to try on. Make a mental note and get the card of the sales clerk that works with you.

Later call the sales clerk (most of whom work on commission and would be happy to sell you something now or later) and ask him or her to write down exactly what your lady was most enamored with.

This then becomes your "stash" for future gift purchases.

Do this at a few reputable jewelry stores and you will eventually have enough potential gifts to last a lifetime!

Keep in mind, however, that styles and tastes do change so be sure to continually update your woman's "wish list."

Now a word about diamonds.

Are they, as the saying goes "a girl's best friend"?

My answer is a resounding "Yes".

Diamonds come in all shapes and sizes, and they are rated for color and clarity.

The color of a diamond tells you how close to perfectly colorless it is. The ratings on color go from "D" down the alphabet, with anything higher than "K" considered pretty good (at least by me).

Clarity refers to the number of occlusions, or imperfections, that are in the diamond. These can only be seen with a magnifying lens. These ratings look like "VS1, VS2, SI1", etc.

Each diamond is also weighed in carats. An average engagement ring would be about 1 carat, with sizes going up as high as 5 carats and beyond.

My dad used to tell the story of the famous "Klopman diamond". Legend has it that the diamond was 25 carats of pure white perfection. Legend also has it, however, that the diamond came with a curse!

When Mrs. Klopman wore the diamond to a New York social event she was asked to explain the curse.

"So exactly what is the curse that comes with this diamond?" she was asked.

"Mr. Klopman!" was her terse reply.

Here is one piece of advice you should always keep in mind when buying diamonds.

SIZE MATTERS!

Whatever you do, don't let anyone convince you that your lady would rather have a small diamond than a big diamond.

Have you ever heard one woman say about another ***"Wow! Did you see the rock on her finger?"***

I bet you have!

Now, have you ever heard one woman say about another *"Wow! Did you see the lack of occlusions in that small diamond on her finger?"*

I doubt it.

Unless the woman carries around a magnifying lens there is no way she can see the occlusions in anybody's diamond, even her own!

So, whenever you have a choice for big or small…GO BIG!

And here is another tip for you when buying diamonds. They come in different shapes.

My son Jonathan, who is a certified diamond rater, explained to me that round diamonds will always be more impressive than any other cut because of the way they refract the light.

And one more thing about buying diamonds. Do not pay full retail.

No matter where you go it is likely that you can negotiate a lower price for the diamond you buy. The diamond business is very competitive and the markups can be very big. So always offer a lower price than what the tag says.

What's the worst that can happen? They say no? Big deal!

But jewelry is not the only thing that will make your woman happy. Here are a few other ideas for special gifts:

A Day of Beauty

Almost every city and town has a day spa that caters to women. A fantastic treat for your woman is a day at the spa, which usually includes a massage, facial, manicure, and pedicure. A special added touch would be for you to take the kids for the day so that she can concentrate only on her own personal needs.

Perfume

The key to buying perfume is to get her what she likes, not what you like.

How do you know the name of what she likes?

That's easy. Just snoop around in her side of the bathroom vanity. You'll see it.

Be sure to take a whiff of what you find to be sure that it is the right stuff. Then write down the name and head for the perfume counter of your local department store.

Sporting Outfits

Does your lady play tennis or golf?

If she does you have an endless supply of gifts to give her. The pro shops in most golf and tennis clubs are stocked with the latest fashions.

And even if you give her the wrong thing, you will get credit for thinking about what she likes to do. All of that stuff can be exchanged

Not sure what size to buy?

The easiest way to find out is to look in her closet.

But some women have a whole series of sizes for different, ahem, "phases" of their body shape.

So here is my advice when you are not sure what size to get.

When it comes to clothes, unlike jewelry, always choose the smaller size.

A very smart man once said *"It is better to be quiet and have people think you are dumb, than it is to open your mouth and confirm that they are correct."*

The same adage holds true here.

It is far better to be wrong on the "small side" because it let's her know that you think of her as a size 6 rather than a size 12. If you buy the big size, even if it is the correct size, you will let her know that you think she is big. And that is never a good thing.

Don't worry. She will exchange it for the right size (and style, and color) but at least you will have sent her a strong message about how she looks to you.

If she says something like "Why did you get me such a small size? You know I am bigger than this!" then your answer should be as swift as it can fly out of your mouth.

"Honey, the sales clerk was a young college girl and I asked her what size she was because to me she looked about the same size as you."

Things NEVER to Buy

No matter how helpful you think you are. No matter how thoughtful, no matter how clever, you should never, ever buy your woman any of the following:

- Vacuum cleaner

- Lawn Mower

- Hair remover

- A TV set that you will end up watching more than she will

- Gift certificates of any kind

- Wrestling tickets (unless she specifically asks for them!)

- Any DVD of the Jerry Springer show

STEP FIVE

Lose the Power Game

"I don't need you to worry for me cause I'm alright
I don't want you to tell me it's time to come home
I don't care what you say anymore, this is my life
Go ahead with your own life, and leave me alone"

Billy Joel

In my "day job" I consult with major corporations to help them set up a dispute resolution system. The system allows an employee who feels that he has been mistreated to have his case heard by a jury of company employees who then have the power to overrule management's decision.

Once managers learn about my system they are generally very supportive. But there is always one cautionary statement that I make to them.

"You will lose some of these cases, not all but some", I tell them. *"As a matter of fact,"* I expound, ***"You have to lose a few!"***

You see, in order for any dispute resolution system to be effective, both sides have to win.

The same thing is true in a marriage or any other relationship.

Over the years I have met many men who like to be "in control" of their family. They want to have the power to determine everything that happens of any consequence, and they are unwilling to share this power with anyone, including their wives.

These men may think they have happy wives, but in most cases they are just deluding themselves.

Among my favorite couples are two doctors from India. Both are brilliant and successful surgeons who have the power of life and death over their patients.

Recently I was talking to the husband, Neri about his relationship with his wife Shushma.

Neri said *"I come from a very traditional Indian family where the husband is the ruler of his family".*

"When Shushma and I got married twenty years ago we discussed things and we both agreed that I, as the man

of the family, would make all of the major decisions in our lives."

With a twinkle in his eye he concluded the story. *"Luckily for me, however, **over the past twenty years there has never been a major decision to be made!"***

Neri is a happy guy, and his wife is happy too.

And we all can learn from Neri.

Rather than get caught up in the power game, Neri has realized how much easier it is to let his wife make a lot of decisions that really don't matter to him.

Does that make Neri a wimp?

Perhaps he is in some eyes but certainly not in mine. In my eyes that makes him a smart guy.

In his book "Don't Sweat the Small Stuff" author Richard Carlson reminds us that

"So many people spend so much of their life energy sweating the small stuff that they completely lose touch with the magic and beauty of life."

Neri will never fit into that category.

So how can you stop "sweating" and make your life a lot easier?

Here are just a few of the complaints I hear from men about their wives, followed by my comments:

Complaint: My wife spends too much money

Comment: How much is peace of mind worth? Do you plan to die with no money left? Is it really worth fighting over a few dollars?

Complaint: The house is too messy

Comment: Keeping the house clean is a family job, not hers alone. Hire a housekeeper, or, if the cost is too high, you help to clean up.

Complaint: Her family bugs me

Comment: Your family probably bugs her too. Accept the fact that they are a part of her life and don't fight about it. Let her have her special time with her family.

Complaint: She doesn't have sex enough with me.

Comment: Take a look in the mirror. Do you see Tom Cruise? For tips about this subject stay tuned for my next book "Happy Hubby's Guide To More and Better Sex"

Complaint: She is always late.

Comment: Don't waste your energy trying to "reform" her. Trust me! The best way to deal with this is to always tell her that she needs to be ready at an earlier time. Then when she is late she will actually be right on time!

Who Makes The Decision?

Let's assume that a decision is about to be made in your household that you can either demand to have the final word on or simply make suggestions and let your wife decide. Let's take an example such as this:

Your wife's mini-van has 140,000 miles and is in need of serious repair. Do you buy a new mini-van, buy a used mini-van, repair the old min-van, or buy something else entirely?"

Some men would consider that a "major decision" and therefore would try to exercise their power as the "man of the family" to dictate what action should be taken.

I would suggest that you take a look at the decision that needs to be made and ask yourself the following questions:

1. Is she just as capable of making this decision as I am?

2. Does this decision mean as much or
    more to her than it does to me?

3. Will this decision have little or
    no effect on me personally?

4. Will she be happier if I just let
    her do what she wants?

5. Will I be happier if I just let
    her do what she wants?

Obviously, if the answer to all of these five questions is "Yes" then the best thing for you to do is to back off and let her make the decision.

But what if the answers are mixed? What if you have one or two "no" answers?

Then you need to ask yourself a tough question. Why are the answers "no"? Is it because I truly believe it and I am justified or is it just my bias coming through.

For example, what if you say "no" to the question "Is my wife just as capable as I am of making this decision?"

Ask yourself why you feel that she is not as capable as you are. Is it because she has made a lot of bad decisions in the past? Or is it because you have been making the decisions for her? Is it her inability that concerns you or is it merely the idea of giving up power?

Take this honest approach with all five questions and you may find that the answer to them all is "Yes".

By letting her make the decision you "lose" the power game. But in reality you "win"

Imagine yourself saying the following to her:

"Honey, I just want you to be happy. If you feel you need a new mini-van that is fine with me. I will be glad to give you advice if you want it but I will support whatever decision you make."

Look for every opportunity to give up the decision making role, maintaining only those decisions that are really important to you. By sharing the decision making "power" and the responsibility you will have a stronger and happier relationship.

Another scenario that often creates problems in marriages is when the husband has the following attitude:

"I do what I want in life. No woman is gonna tell me what to do! No way I'm gonna be whipped!"

You meet guys like this at bars, NASCAR races, bowling lanes, and in all other places where men like to hang out.

Heaven forbid one of them was to say, *"sorry guys I gotta go now. My wife wants me home to help get the kids to bed."*

What kind of abuse would that poor guy take from his "macho" peers? You can imagine!

So how then does a man deal with a woman who wants and needs him at home when he would rather be out "playing with his buddies"?

My best advice is this:

Do not set yourself up for this scenario.

Spend time with your woman talking about the "comfort zone" for each of you.

The "comfort zone" is what each of you can tolerate from the other and still be happy.

For example, you probably agree that, even though you are in love you both can use time with your friends.

Talk about what that means and what limits should be set for each of you to stay happy. Then test the plan and tweak it until you have reached your "comfort zone."

Here is an example:

Fred knows that Sally is okay with him playing golf one weekend day each week but not two. If the kids have a game on Saturday then Fred will be sure to play golf on Sunday.

Once in while if there is a two day tournament on Saturday and Sunday then Sally will be okay with that.

This plan becomes an agreement between two loving people, not one person dominating the other.

Fred could just ignore Sally and do whatever he wants. That option is always open to him.

But he doesn't do that.

Why?

Not because he is a wimp. Not because he is afraid of Sally.

Fred does it because he knows that agreement makes Sally happy!

And Fred is happy too.

Once the plan is put into place then there is no reason to fight about it. There is also no reason to deliberately break the agreement without discussing it first.

These same limitations will apply to Sally as well.

So a truly happy couple will take whatever time they need to work out the details of their arrangement. Some even put them in writing!

Whatever approach you use, remember that the race through life is a marathon, not a sprint. Winning unnecessary battles may make you feel good for a short time, but in the long run they could cost you the race.

STEP SIX

Listen…No…Really Listen to Her

Some day when we're dreaming,
Deep In love, not a lot to say
Then we will remember
Things we said today.

The Beatles

Communication between men and women is probably the most over analyzed subject I have ever seen.

Every Woman's magazine, every self-help book, and television shows from Oprah to Dr Phil constantly cover the subject.

So in this chapter I will try to tell you a few things that you may not have heard before.

Rule number one when communicating with your woman is very simple:

Put down the sports page, look her in the eye, and listen to what she has to say.

No, I mean really listen!

See if you can relate to this conversation between Mike and Cathy over the breakfast table:

Cathy: *Mike the guest toilet was plugged up.*

Mike (reading): *Uh huh*

Cathy: *The water spilled all over the floor.*

Mike (still reading): *That's nice*

Cathy: *It leaked through the floor and ruined the ceiling of the dining room.*

Mike (still reading): *Good, good.*

Cathy: *I called the plumber and he came yesterday.*

Mike (still reading): *Good idea honey.*

Cathy: *And after he fixed the toilet he and I had wild passionate sex on our bed.*

Mike (still reading): *That's great honey!*

One hour later Cathy received a call from Mike.

Mike: **What did you say about the plumber?**

Cathy: *Nothing dear.*

Can you relate to this?

One key to making any woman happy is to get to know her. What is it that makes her tick? What makes her laugh? What makes her cry? What does she find good about your relationship and what would she like to be better?

This will only happen if you are willing to really listen to her.

In my effective listening class one of the things I talk about with my students is the fact that there are four basic forms of communication:

Reading

Writing

Talking

Listening

Of the four, guess which one we do the most. You got it…Listening!

And guess which one is the only one that we are never taught how to do.

Right again...Listening!

We often assume that, because we know how to hear, that means we automatically know how to listen. But hearing and listening are different.

Hearing is not a skill. It is a sense, just like sight, taste, touch, and smell.

Listening, on the other hand, is a skill. It can be taught and it can be learned.

If you want to be a good listener for the woman in your life to talk to here are some key things that you must do:

- Make sure the atmosphere is conducive to good listening. Turn off the TV, put down the newspaper, and turn off the cell phones. Make this conversation the most important thing in your life for however long it takes.

- Give the lady your conscious attention. Establish eye contact and maintain it. Did you ever try to talk to somebody who isn't looking at you? How does that make you feel? Like they are not interested in what you have to say?

- The way you sit can make a big difference. If your woman is talking to you and you are sitting with both your arms and legs crossed you are sending a subtle but strong message that you are not accepting what she has to say.

- Your facial expression speaks volumes about how you are receiving her words. If you roll your eyes, or grin sarcastically while she is talking to you then you are saying that either you do not believe her or that you think what she is saying is dumb.

- Try not to get excited too early by what she is saying. Early over-involvement in the content or point of view causes you to become preoccupied with your own reactions or responses. If you do this then you will begin thinking about what your response will be and this will cause you to miss the rest of what she has to say.

- Keep an open mind. Don't let your emotional reactions to the lady's words turn you on or off to what is being said, especially if those words are critical of something you have done or said.

- Let her finish what she has to say uninterrupted. You will have plenty of opportunity to get your words in. Remember, if your goal is to make her happy then you should focus on listening, not talking.

- If you have difficulty keeping quiet here is a tip I learned from my old friend Bob. Place your index finger over lips while she is talking. This will require you to move the finger before you can talk, and that alone will keep reminding you to let her finish what she has to say.

- After she has finished speaking then you should paraphrase what your understanding is about what she has just said. An example of paraphrasing would be this:

"Honey, I think what I am hearing you say is that you are disappointed in Billy's grades and you want me to take a more active role to make sure he gets his homework done right. Is that what you mean?"

She will either confirm what she meant or restate it. But either way you will be sure to have a communication connection.

Responding to Criticism

More truth in advertising here, fellas. This is the one area that my wife would tell you I am not so good at!

I can tell you what we are supposed to do, but I must admit that it is difficult at best for me.

Let us assume for a moment that you have just listened patiently while your lady has unloaded on you about what a slob you are.

Now it is your turn to speak.

Here is the most important piece of information I can give you at this point.

Avoid a defensive reaction!

What is the natural reaction when someone tells you that you are messy?

Try this one:

"Me messy? What are you talking about? You're the one that messes things up around here! And another thing, we haven't had sex in two weeks! So there! Take that!!

This would be bad right now but then, if you are really defensive, you can add the final blow:

"And you talk about slobs, what about that fat slob mother of yours? I bet she's the one who put you up to this!"

Feel better? Perhaps momentarily.

But guess what? You will eventually end up apologizing for what you said. And the damage could take years to mend.

Here is an alternative approach that will work a lot better:

"Honey, I can understand why you feel the way you do about this. I realize that having a clean house is very important to you."

Comment: By acknowledging that she is justified in her feelings you have not plead guilty. You have simply accepted her right to feel badly about this topic.

"If you are unhappy about this then I am not happy either, because I care about you and your feelings."

Comment: At this point she should be ready to touch, so an arm around the shoulder should be accepted readily.

"I would like to work with you to find a way to make things better for you. So let's both sleep on it tonight and let's come up with a plan of action tomorrow."

Comment: This allows for a "cooling down" period and buys you the time you need to think of a way to resolve the issue.

By the way, my experience has shown that often this will be the end of the discussion. By simply acknowledging her right to feel the way she does it is quite possible that she will be ready to move on without any further discussion.

At least until the next time you mess the house up!

QUIZ

Now is the time to see how much you have learned. Take this quiz and then score yourself on how happy you will make your woman.

1. You are at a dress shop when your wife comes out of the dressing room. She is wearing a red dress and holding the same dress in pink. "I love both of these colors," she says, "Which one should I buy?"

    Your response is:

    A. Don't you have enough dresses already?

    B. Either one would look good

    C. They are so pretty on you I think you should buy them both!

2. You come home from work and your wife is waiting for you with a "honey do list" for next weekend. Your plan for next weekend was to do

nothing more than "veg out" watching football games.

Your response is:

A. Which part of N F L don't you understand, woman?

B. How about if I do it next week?

C. I would be happy to do whatever it takes. I'll work out a schedule that gets what you need done and still gives me the time I need to watch football.

3. Your lady says that you don't have enough in common.

   Your Response is:

   A. We made two kids so I guess we must have something in common!

   B. Let me teach you how to play poker.

   C. I'm so happy you said that. Let's find a few things that we can do together, just the two of us.

4. You are about to go out to a fancy "black tie affair. Your lady comes out of the bathroom dressed in a

floor length gown. "Do I look fat in this dress?" she asks.

Your Response is:

A. Is the Pope Catholic?

B. Turn around...hmmm...no not really.

C. Fat? Are you kidding me? (arms around her) You will be the most stunning woman at the party tonight...just like you always are!

5. Your best friend and his wife are getting divorced. Your wife asks you if you think that could ever happen to you.

    Your Response is:

    A. Not after I saw how much it cost my buddy.

    B. That's something I have never even thought about.

    C. I promised to love you until death do us part. And I love you more today than the day I married you. Nothing could ever change that.

6. Your mother-in-law is coming to stay for a week at your house. Your wife asks what you will do while she is visiting.

Your Response is:

A. Do the words "Holiday Inn" ring a bell?

B. I'll be around if you need me.

C. I want to take you and your mom out to her favorite restaurant Saturday night.

SCORING

Score yourself as follows:

0 points for each A. answer

1 point for each B. answer

2 points for each C. answer

YOUR SCORE:

10-12 points: Congratulations! You are well equipped to make your woman happy.

6-9 points: your heart is in the right place, but you still are a work in progress.

5 points or less: Turn to page 1

ABOUT THE AUTHOR

HARVEY CARAS is president of CARAS & ASSOCIATES, INC., a Clarksville, MD based consulting firm specializing in Alternative Dispute Resolution Systems which he founded in 1985. His list of over 1,000 clients includes Alcoa, Armstrong, BASF, Best Buy, Dana, Darden, Dupont, Federated Department Stores, Ford Motor Company, GE, Johnson Controls, Hershey Foods, Iron Mountain, Kodak, Kraft, Marriott, Mead, Rockwell, Rubbermaid, Pillsbury, Sprint, NBC, Toyota, Westinghouse, International Paper, and the U.S. Department of Homeland Security.

A native of Malden, Massachusetts, Harvey graduated from Tufts University in 1970. He then completed over 15 years in the Human Resource Management field with General Electric. In 1982 he developed the Peer Review Dispute Resolution system, which Harvard Business School Press has called *"the most cloned procedure for resolving complaints in U.S. manufacturing - and possibly in all industry."*

Harvey's work has been highlighted by *HR Magazine*, *Business Week*, *Industry-Week*, the *Wall Street Journal*, *Personnel Administrator*, *Personnel Journal*,

The Washington Post, and many other national publications.

In May, 1990 Harvey was part of a contingent of US Human Resources professionals which traveled to the Soviet Union to present American management techniques to their Soviet counterparts. Harvey delivered a presentation on the subject of Alternative Dispute Resolution to the Soviet Academy of Arts and Sciences.

He currently resides with his wife Joanne in Clarksville, Maryland and Port St Lucie, Florida. They have been married since 1982 and have three children; Jonathan, who lives in Israel with his wife Sarah; Rachel, who attends Lehigh University and will attend Logan Chiropractic College beginning in 2007; and Mickey, a high school senior who will continue his studies in Israel in 2007.

Printed in the United States
70693LV00001B/164